First World War
and Army of Occupation
War Diary
France, Belgium and Germany

57 DIVISION
172 Infantry Brigade
Royal Munster Fusiliers
1st Battalion
1 May 1918 - 31 May 1919

WO95/2985/1

The Naval & Military Press Ltd
www.nmarchive.com
Published in association with The National Archives

Published by

The Naval & Military Press Ltd

Unit 10 Ridgewood Industrial Park,

Uckfield, East Sussex,

TN22 5QE England

Tel: +44 (0) 1825 749494

www.naval-military-press.com

www.nmarchive.com

This diary has been reprinted in facsimile from the original. Any imperfections are inevitably reproduced and the quality may fall short of modern type and cartographic standards.

© **Crown Copyright**
Images reproduced by permission of The National Archives, London, England, 2015.

Contents

Document type	Place/Title	Date From	Date To
Heading	WO95/2985/1 57 Div 172 Inf Brig 1bn Royal Munster Fus 1918 May 1919 May		
Heading	57th Division 172nd Infy Bde 1st Bn Royal Minister Fusiliers May 1918-May 1919 From 16 Div 47 Bde)		
War Diary	Henu	01/05/1918	04/05/1918
War Diary	Gommecourt	05/05/1918	12/05/1918
War Diary	Gommecourt Wood	14/05/1918	23/05/1918
War Diary	Chateau De La Haie	29/05/1918	31/05/1918
Operation(al) Order(s)	Operation Order by Lieut Colonel R.R. Kane D.S.O. Comdg 1st R Munster Fusiliers	04/05/1918	04/05/1918
Operation(al) Order(s)	Operation Orders No.16 by Lieut Colonel R.R. Kane D.S.O. Comdg 1st R Munster Fusiliers	28/05/1918	28/05/1918
War Diary	Henu	01/05/1918	05/05/1918
War Diary	Gommecourt	06/05/1918	31/05/1918
War Diary	Right Sub Sector Left Sector	01/06/1918	14/06/1918
War Diary	Couin	15/06/1918	15/06/1918
War Diary	Left Sub Sector Of Right Sector	24/06/1918	24/06/1918
War Diary	Gommecourt	29/06/1918	29/06/1918
Miscellaneous	Daily Strengths For June 1918		
Operation(al) Order(s)	Operation Orders No.20 by Lt Col R.R.G. Kane D.S.O. Comdg 1st Royal Munster Fus	13/06/1918	13/06/1918
Operation(al) Order(s)	Operation Orders No.21 by Lieut Colonel R.R. Kane D.S.O. Comdg 1st R Munster Fusiliers	21/06/1918	21/06/1918
War Diary	Gommecourt	01/07/1918	02/07/1918
War Diary	Authie	03/07/1918	28/07/1918
War Diary	Saulty	29/07/1918	29/07/1918
War Diary	Etrun	30/07/1918	16/08/1918
Miscellaneous	1st Bn. Royal Munster Fusrs Daily Strength Of Battn		
Operation(al) Order(s)	Operation Orders No. 22 by Lieut Colonel R.R. Kane D.S.O. Comdg 1st R Munster Fusiliers	30/06/1918	30/06/1918
Operation(al) Order(s)	Operation Orders No. 23 By Major G.W. Nightingale M.C Comdg.	15/07/1918	15/07/1918
Miscellaneous	Operation Orders By Major G.W. Nightingale M.C Comdg. 1st Batt The Roy Munster Fus	25/07/1918	25/07/1918
Miscellaneous	Operation Orders By Major G.W. Nightingale M.C Comdg. 1st Batt The Roy Munster Fus	26/07/1918	26/07/1918
Operation(al) Order(s)	Operation Orders By Lt. Col R.R.G. Kane DSO. Comdg 1st Bn Royal Munster Fus	31/07/1918	31/07/1918
War Diary	Etrun	01/08/1918	01/08/1918
War Diary	Arras	02/08/1918	02/08/1918
War Diary	Athies	02/08/1918	08/08/1918
War Diary	Wakefield Camp	09/08/1918	17/08/1918
War Diary	Frevillers	18/08/1918	21/08/1918
War Diary	Noyelle Remy	22/08/1918	22/08/1918
War Diary	Grouches	23/08/1918	23/08/1918
War Diary	Bavincourt	24/08/1918	24/08/1918
War Diary	Ronsart	25/08/1918	26/08/1918
War Diary	Ficheux	27/08/1918	27/08/1918
War Diary	Heninel	28/08/1918	28/08/1918
War Diary	Martin Sur Jeuil	29/08/1918	31/08/1918

Type	Description	From	To
Miscellaneous	Officer's Casualties		
Miscellaneous	Honours Gained During The Month Of Sept 1918	00/09/1918	00/09/1918
Miscellaneous	Appendix L.I (c)	28/08/1918	28/08/1918
War Diary	Tunnel Trench (W. Of Fontaine La Croissilles)	01/09/1918	02/09/1918
War Diary	Drocourt Queant Switch Due E of Riencourt	02/09/1918	02/09/1918
War Diary	Tunnel Trench	03/09/1918	12/09/1918
War Diary	Moeuvres	12/09/1918	16/09/1918
War Diary	Bullecourt	16/09/1918	16/09/1918
War Diary	Baileulmont	17/09/1918	18/09/1918
War Diary	Lagnicourt	25/09/1918	27/09/1918
War Diary	Gantaing	27/09/1918	30/09/1918
War Diary	Proville	30/09/1918	30/09/1918
War Diary	La Folie Wood	01/10/1918	05/10/1918
War Diary	Proville	06/10/1918	08/10/1918
War Diary	Cambrai	09/10/1918	09/10/1918
War Diary	Anneux	09/10/1918	10/10/1918
War Diary	Boursies	11/10/1918	11/10/1918
War Diary	Hermies	12/10/1918	12/10/1918
War Diary	Bethune	13/10/1918	13/10/1918
War Diary	Vaudricourt	13/10/1918	14/10/1918
War Diary	La Touquet	14/10/1918	15/10/1918
War Diary	Raddingham	16/10/1918	16/10/1918
War Diary	Fin De La Guerre	17/10/1918	17/10/1918
War Diary	Sequedin	17/10/1918	19/10/1918
War Diary	Le Marais	20/10/1918	20/10/1918
War Diary	Lille	21/10/1918	21/10/1918
War Diary	Ascq	21/10/1918	21/10/1918
War Diary	Willems	22/10/1918	24/10/1918
War Diary	Cornet	25/10/1918	25/10/1918
War Diary	Honnevain	28/10/1918	31/10/1918
Miscellaneous	1st Bn. Royal Munster Fusiliers	00/10/1918	00/10/1918
War Diary	Fauberg De Fives Lille	01/11/1918	30/11/1918
War Diary	Lille	01/12/1918	03/12/1918
War Diary	Carvin	04/12/1918	04/12/1918
War Diary	Maroeuil	05/12/1918	31/01/1919
Miscellaneous	1st Batt The Royal Munster Fusiliers	00/01/1919	00/01/1919
War Diary	Maroeuil	03/01/1919	30/04/1919
War Diary	Maroeuil France	01/05/1919	31/05/1919

WO 95 2985/1

57 Div 172 Inf Brig
1 Bn Royal Munster Fus.
1916 May - 1919 May

57TH DIVISION
172ND INFY BDE

1ST BN ROYAL MUNSTER FUSILIERS

MAY 1918 - MAY 1919

(FROM 16 DIV 47 BDE)

1st Bn Royal Munster Fusiliers

Page I

WAR DIARY
or
INTELLIGENCE SUMMARY

Place	Date	Hour	Summary of Events and Information	Remarks and references to Appendices
HENU	1918 MAY 1st to 4th May		The Battalion billeted in HENU. Parades from 9am till 1pm. All companies had the use of the ranges at some time during the last 4 days. Brigade Tactical exercise on the afternoon of the 4th May.	
GOMMECOURT	5.5.18		At 2 p.m. the details of the Bn, 370 strong, marched to MARIEUX under Major Nightingale, & joined the 57th Divisional hing. The remainder of the Bn, proceeded at 5 p.m. to FONQUEVILLERS where they met guides from the 42nd Division, who led the companies into their respective positions, the distribution of the companies being one company in the front line, one coy. in close support, one coy. in support & one coy. in reserve. Bn. HQ are in GOMMECOURT village.	
	6.5.18 to 11.5.18		Everything was normal & quiet & nothing to report. Inter company reliefs carried out, but otherwise uneventful.	
	11.5.18	7 p.m.	The enemy opened up a heavy bombardment of gas shells on FONQUEVILLERS. The Bn. was not affected, except for the transport, which was bringing up the rations, & sustained two casualties both very slight. The village was placed out of bounds for 5 days.	
	12.5.18 & 13.5.18		Very quiet period. All these days were passing test & there was very little activity on either side.	
GOMMECOURT WOOD	14.5.18	9 p.m.	The Bn. was relieved in the front line by the 9th KING'S LIVERPOOL REGT. & took up its positions as Reserve Battn. in trenches forming the defences of GOMMECOURT WOOD.	

1st Bn Royal Munster Fusiliers

Page II

Army Form C. 2118.

WAR DIARY
or
INTELLIGENCE SUMMARY.
(Erase heading not required.)

Place	Date	Hour	Summary of Events and Information	Remarks and references to Appendices
GOMMECOURT	15.5.18		The Battalion completed its relief about 2am & stood to arms shortly afterwards. The day was spent in reconnoitring the new battle position. All Coy Commanders rehearsed the defence scheme. Two coys went out on working parties at 9.30pm. One working on RUM TRENCH the other digging on GOMMECOURT TRENCH. The work was skilled. Relief began in the morning & one hour in the evening. Only one man wounded.	
WOOD	16.5.18		The day was uneventful. Three Coys were out working at night. One was working with R.E. Supervision during the day. The transport was shelled bringing up rations in the FONQUEVILLERS — GOMMECOURT road. No casualty.	
	17 to 19 5/18		Uneventful, except for intermittent shelling, & some sniping in the wood.	
	20.5.18		Considerable enemy shelling working parties as usual. Stood to arms in battle positions from 2am to 5am as there was evidence of an enemy attack.	
	21.5.18		Stood to arms again tonight & this night, as enemy were supposed to be attacking. Nothing developed, but fairly heavily shelled.	
	22.5.18		Bn relieved in GOMMECOURT WOOD Sector by the 2/7 KINGS LIVERPOOL REGT. Disposition of coys; Two coys in BEER TRENCH, 1/2 FONQUEVILLERS, two in reserve at CHATEAU DE LA HAYE. Bn H.Q. at the latter place at first. Later in BEER TRENCH.	
	23.5.18 to 29.5.18		This period quiet was uneventful. Return coys in BEER TRENCH were relieved on the 26.5.18 & became	

1st Royal Munster Fusiliers

Part III

Army Form C. 2118.

WAR DIARY
or
INTELLIGENCE SUMMARY.
(Erase heading not required.)

Instructions regarding War Diaries and Intelligence Summaries are contained in F. S. Regs., Part II. and the Staff Manual respectively. Title pages will be prepared in manuscript.

Place	Date	Hour	Summary of Events and Information	Remarks and references to Appendices
CHÂTEAU DE LA HAIE	29.5.18		contines	
	30.5.18		Took to CHÂTEAU DE LA HAIE. 2/5 K.O. Borderers Rgt.	
			The Bn. relieved the corresponding Bn. in the right subsector of the left sector. Disposition as follows. Two coys in the front line, One in Support, One in reserve.	
	31.5.18		Bn. settled down in new line. Day quiet except occasional shelling.	

SECRET.

OPERATION ORDER

BY No. 12

LIEUT.COLONEL. H.H.KAHN, D.S.O. COMDG. 1st R.MUNSTER FUSILIERS.

IN the FIELD. 4th MAY, 1918.

Reference MAP. 27-B- N.E. 1/20,000

1. The Battalion will relieve 1/6th MANCHESTER Regiment on the left of the RIGHT SECTION of the BUSNES DIVISION-AL AREA of the IVth CORPS FRONT, on the night of the 5/6th MAY, 1918, as under :-

    "W"Coy will relieve Front Line   (C)Coy 1/6th Manchesters.
    X. "   "   "   Close Support(A) "   -do-
    Y. "   "   "   Support.   (D) "   -do-
    Z. "   "   "   Reserve.   (B) "   -do-

2. Officers and other ranks detailed to proceed to the Line will parade on the Parade Ground ready to march off at 6.p.m. 5th instant.

3. Details for personnel remaining out of the line will be issued later.

4. The u/m Advance Party will proceed to Line and report to Adjutant,6th Bn.Manchester Regt.by 6.p.m.to-day. They will reconnoitre the Battalion Front by night :-
2/Lieut.J.HIGGINS, 1 Officer from each Coy, 1 Sergt.from each Platoon. Nos 1 & 2 Lewis Gun Teams with Ammunition Horse, 1/Cpl.Desmond and 1 N.C.O. Headquarters. This party will parade at H.Q.Mess at 5.p.m. today.

5. Guides from 6th Battalion,Manchester Regt (1 per Platoon) will be at ..... CHURCH at 9.15.p.m. 5th instant.

6. Bn.H.Q. will close at ..... at 6.p.m. and open as soon after as possible at N.30.d.5.1.

7. Lewis Gunners will carry 50 rounds S.A.A. all other ranks 120 rounds S.A.A. Greatcoats will be carried.

8. All Blankets, Packs, etc, will be stacked at Q.M's Stores at 2.p.m. tomorrow. All Officers Kits,etc, will be stacked at same place by 1.p.m. tomorrow.

9. All Defence Schemes,Maps,Photographs,etc; concerning the the Line will be taken over, and copies of receipts sent to Intelligence Officer by 10.a.m. 6th instant. Captain.T.J.Lee.M.C. will hand over all schemes,etc,to incoming Unit. All Trench Stores etc,will be taken over; copies of Trench Store List to Bn.H.Q.by 11.a.m.6th inst.

10. Transport Officer will arrange for following (Coys please note):- 2 Limbers,Lewis Gun at Bn.H.Q. 5.p.m.
    Mess Cart,Maltese Cart.
    C.O's.Adjut's & 4 Coy Officers Horses.) 5.30.p.m.

11. Transport lines, ..Stores and Orderly Room(to deal with all Routine matters) will be taken over at ....., by Transport Officer, from 6th Manchester Regt.Route via ...... Advance Parties from each of above will proceed to ...... at 10.a.m.5th inst.to take over. Receipt for all tents taken over and a cleanliness certificate will be sent Bn.H.Q. by noon 6th instant.

12. Advance Parties of 6th Manchester Regt will take over Billets in ..... All lines will be left scrupulously clean. Copies of receipts for all tents,etc,will be sent to Rear Bde.H.Q. (N.9.a.3.8)by 12noon 6th instant.

13. Completion of relief will be wired Bn.H.Q. by O.C's COMDG. (Ruy. ..16. HOURS). as soon as possible.

H.Mander Captain, A/Adjutant.

PTO

COPIES TO :-

No. 1. C.O.
2. 2nd in Command.
3. O.C. T.M.G. Coys.
4. Intelligence Officer.
5. Qr-Master.
6. Transport Officer.
7. H.Q. 172nd Inf. Bde.
8. O.C. 6th Manchester Regt.
9. R.S.M.
10. & 11. War Diary.
12. File.

S E C R E T.   COPY NO. 9
O P E R A T I O N   O R D E R S - No. 16.
BY
LIEUT.COLONEL.R.R.KANE, D.S.O.COMDG, 1st R.MUNSTER FUSILIERS.
IN the FIELD.   28th MAY, 1918.
==

(1) The Battalion will relieve the 2/5th Bn.K.O.R.L.R. in
    the Right Sector of the LEFT SECTION of the Divisional
    Front on the night 29/30th MAY, 1918.

2. "X" Coy will relieve "B" Coy K.O.R.L.R. (Right Front).
    "Z" "   -do-   "C" "   -do-   (Left   ").
    "Y" "   -do-   "D" "   -do-   (Support).
    "W" "   -do-   "A" "   -do-   (Reserve)

3. Relief will commence at undermentioned times :-
    "X" Coy will leave CHATEAU de la HAIE at 9.15.p.m.
    "Z" "   -do-   -do-   " 10. p.m.
    "Y" "   -do-   ROSSIGNOL FARM   " 9.30.p.m.
    "W" "   -do-   -do-   " 10.10.p.m.
    Distances of 100 yards between Platoons and 200 yards be-
    tween Companies to be strictly observed.

4. Guides at the rate of 1 per Platoon will be at Junction
    AILETTE TR. BUCQUEVILLERS-COIGNEUCOURT ROAD, B.29.c.05.80.
    at 10-15.p.m.

5. ADVANCE PARTIES. Tonight the following Advance Parties will
    proceed to the Line to take over :- 1 Officer per Coy,
    1 Sergeant per Platoon, 2 men from each L.Gun Team.
    One representative of each Section in Forward Posts.(i.e.
    4 Posts "X" Coy, 8 Posts "Z" Coy).
    Guides for these parties at the rate of one per Coy will
    be at B.29.c.05.80. (as above) at 9.15.p.m.

6. "W" Coy will detail one Subaltern, who will be in charge
    of S.A.A. and dumps, to report to Battn.Int.Officer at
    at Bn.H.Q.- 9-45.p.m.29th, to proceed to Line.

7. All Lewis Gun Ammunition will be taken in Line with
    Advance Parties tonight. Each man, except Lewis Gunners,
    will carry 120.Rounds.S.A.A. L.Gunners will carry 50 Rounds.

8. All Packs will be stacked at respective Coy.H.Q.by 6.p.m.
    tonight. Greatcoats will be taken to the Line with men.

9. All Defence Schemes,Trench Stores,etc, will be taken and
    handed over. Copies of receipts to be at Bn.H.Q.by 10.a.m.
    30th instant.

10. Advance Parties from 2/5 K.O.R.L.R. may be expected to-
    morrow. All Billets will be handed over clean, and a
    receipt for cleanliness obtained.

11. Completion of relief will be wired at once to Battn.H.Q.
    (B.8.a.15.05) by CODE WORDS - M.13.HOTED.)

12. Transport Officer will arrange following Transport :-
    28th - Taking Packs (referred to in para.8.) to Q.M.Stores.
    28th.- Conveying L.G.Ammunition (re.para.7) from Coys at
    5.p.m. and handing to Advance Parties at LONE TREE at
    9.30.p.m. (Companies Please Note). One Subaltern from
    "Y"Coy will be responsible for seeing above carried out,
    and will report to T.O. COIGNEUX at 6.30.p.m.
    29th - One Limber per Coy at Coy H.Q. and 1 Bn.H.Q. 8.30.p.m.
    Mess Cart at Battn.H.Q. at 7.p.m.

13. A C K N O W L E D G E.

ISSUED AT 2.30.p.m.28-5-18.   (Sd) C.W.KANE-DEW,Captain,

                                         A/Adjutant,1st R.Munster Fusiliers.

```
COPY No.  1  to   C.O.
  -do-    2.      172. Infantry Bde.
  -do-    3.      2/5th K.O.R.L.R.
  -do-    4.      "W" Coy
  -do-    5.      "Y"  "
  -do-    6.      "X"  "
  -do-    7.      "Z"  "
  -do-    8.      T.O. & Qr-M.
  -do-    9.      Int. officer.
  -do-   10.      Sig. officer.
  -do-   11.      R.S.M.
  -do-   12-13-   War Diary.
  -do-   14.      Office.
```

1st Rhodesia Fusiliers — Attached KRRC

WAR DIARY or INTELLIGENCE SUMMARY.

Army Form C. 2118.

PAGE IV

Place	Date	Hour	Trench Strength Officers	Trench Strength Other Ranks	Details (Marieux) Officers	Details Other Ranks	Casualties Officers	Casualties O.Rs.	Reinforcements Officers	Reinforcements O.Rs.	To Hospital	Total Officers	Total O.R.
HENU		1st	39	1143	1	1	1	12				40	1109
HENU		2nd	39	1109						3	1	39	1109
HENU		3rd	39	1096							14	39	1096
		4th	39	1100								39	1100
		5th	39	1105								39	1104
		6th	39	1107								39	1107
GOMMECOURT		7th	22	589	18	523				13		40	1115
		8th	22	585	19	528						40	1113
		9th	21	586	19	525		4			1	40	1111
		10th	21	584	19	521						40	1105
		11th	21	580	17	510		4				38	1090
		12th	21	580	16	485						38	1065
		13th	21	578	16	485		4				37	1063
		14th	21	575	16	485						37	1060
		15th	21	576	16	484		2				37	1060
		16th	21	575	16	490		4		5		37	1065
		17th	21	581	19	495		2				40	1076
		18th	20	580	18	505		2			15	38	1085
		19th	20	580	19	504		4			2	39	1084
		20th	23	548	17	540		5	1	9		40	1088
		21st	22	562	15	524		4				37	1086
		22nd	22	562	15	524						37	1086
		23rd	22	563	18	515		4		13		40	1091
		24th	21	562	19	512		2				40	1074
		25th	20	575	17	535		4		20		37	1110
		26th	18	565	17	550		2				35	1115
		27th	21	545	18	548		4			3	39	1113
		28th	22	552	18	522		3		15		40	1114
		29th	22	553	18	515		2				40	1118
		30th	19	564	21	446					4	40	1118
		31st	19	565	21	552		1				40	1118

1st Bn Royal Munster Fusiliers

Page I

HEADQUARTERS
No. 2619
-3 JUL 1918
The Royal Munster Fusiliers

WAR DIARY
or
INTELLIGENCE SUMMARY.
(Erase heading not required.)

Army Form C. 2118.

Instructions regarding War Diaries and Intelligence Summaries are contained in F. S. Regs., Part II. and the Staff Manual respectively. Title pages will be prepared in manuscript.

Place	Date	Hour	Summary of Events and Information	Remarks and references to Appendices
Left Sub-Sector Left Sector	1/6/18 to 5/6/18		1/6/18 Bn in the front-line, holding the right sub-sector & the left sector. Dispositions of Bn: two companies in front line (X & Z coys) 1 coy in support (Y coy) & 1 coy in reserve (W coy). Inter-company relief every 4 days. Period from 1.6.18 to 13.6.18 was quiet. No operations on either side. Very few casualties — about 16 in all including 1 officer (Capt Wrentham). On the morning of the 7th June, the S.O.S. signal was put up, as an enemy raid was expected. The front line was heavily shelled with gas shells throughout. Remainder of the Brig lifted to the support lines. No developments followed. Remainder of the day was very quiet.	
"	13/6/18		Ressignol Wood was fired on by our own artillery with a view to setting it on fire, which was unsuccessful. Slight retaliation by the enemy, in neighbourhood of CHATEAU DE LA HAIE & FONQUEVILLERS. Front line heavily bombarded at about 5 p.m. An infantry attack. The Bn was relieved at 11 pm by the 2/4 Bn S. Lancs Regt. See Appendix II	
COUIN	15/6/18	6.25 pm	Bn arrived in COUIN, where it remained in Divisional reserve for 8 days.	
Left Sub-Sector Right Sector	24/6/18		Bn relieved the 2/7 K.O.R.L. Regt. in the left Subsector of the right sector with H.Qtrs at BONNECOURT, & remained in the sector for 8 days.	

1st Royal Munster Fusiliers   Part III   Army Form C. 2118.

WAR DIARY
or
INTELLIGENCE SUMMARY.

(Erase heading not required.)

Place	Date	Hour	Summary of Events and Information	Remarks and references to Appendices
SOMMECOURT	6/8/18		Minor operation took place in Rossignol Wood. Advance posts withdrawn for the purpose. The post destroyed by enemy shell fire - inventory (?) of 1 L.G. & Lyon - 1 man killed & 5 wounded. Otherwise very quiet during the month. A statement of stores lost at MYPEUX [?].	

(signed) W.H. Shepherd Major
Comdg 1st R.M. Fus

Daily Strengths for June 1915

Date	Strength O.R.			Sick O.R.	Details O.R.			Remarks
1	1123	30	580	17	512	—	—	
2	1116	30	577	18	490	1	1	
3	1104	30	576	18	521	1	1	
4	1102	40	588	20	514	1	1	
5	1105	40	585	14	518	1	3	
6	1100	40	560	20	520	—	—	
7	1095	40	560	20	475	—	—	
8	1089	40	577	20	472	—	—	
9	1080	40	540	20	515	—	—	
10	1099	40	560	10	604	—	23	
11	1090	40	586	20	502	—	—	
12	1091	30	510	20	525	—	1	
13	1090	30	565	19	520	—	2	
14	1091	20	552	10	545	1	—	
15	1201	40	441	10	455	—	3	
16	1081	40	454	14	452	—	2	
17	1090	40	450	15	486	—	3	
18	1081	40	464	11	458	—	—	
19	1084	40	452	11	542	—	1	
20	1024	20	441	20	515	—	—	
21	1022	20	580	20	454	1	1	
22	1018	20	715	12	441	—	—	
23	1018	41	693	15	457	—	—	
24	1001	45	693	15	854	—	6	
25	985	45	647	25	464	—	—	
26	990	46	575	27	497	—	10	0.83

SECRET. COPY No.......

O P E R A T I O N O R D E R S. No.

by

Lt. Col. [illegible] D.S.O. Comdg. 1st. Royal Munster Fusiliers.
In the Field [illegible]

---

1. The Battalion will be relieved on night of 14/15 th. Inst. by 2/7th. Bn. [illegible] commencing about 11 p.m.

2. [illegible] Coy. R.Munster Fus. will be relieved by [illegible] Coy. [illegible]
[illegible] " " " [illegible] " "
[illegible] " " " [illegible] " "
[illegible] " " " [illegible] " "

3. Advance parties from [illegible] will proceed to line on morning of 14th. Inst. to take over.

4. The following guides will report to 2nd. Lieut. O'Reilly at Battn. Hd. Qrs. at 9 p.m. 1 per platoon, 1 Hd. Qr. Coy.. They will guide incoming platoons from junction [illegible] C.T. and [illegible] ROAD to the line.

5. All trench stores, Defence Schemes etc. will be handed over. Copies of receipts to reach Bn. H.Qrs. by noon 15th. Inst.. Certificate of cleanliness will be obtained also.

6. All Gum Boots will be returned to Bn. H.Qrs. by noon 14th. Inst. All Hot Food Containers will be handed over. Qr.Master will arrange to hand over all Petrol Tins in excess of Mobile ~~[illegible]~~ Reserve Establishment.

7. On completion of relief Battalion will proceed to [illegible] and take over from 2/6th. Bn. [illegible] (Hd.Qrs. at [illegible])
Route via [illegible].
Intervals of 200 yards between companies and 100 yards between platoons will be observed.
[illegible] Coys. will take over from [illegible] respectively.

8. The following advance parties will proceed to [illegible] tomorrow morning (14th. Inst.) at 9 a.m. to take over:- 1 officer per company, 1 N.C.O. per platoon. 2nd.Lieut. Gordon and 1 N.C.O. Hd. Qr. Coy.

9. All documents etc. will be taken over and receipts given for same.

10 The following details will report at Bn. H.Qrs. at 9 a.m. 15th. Inst. for duties in [illegible] :- 2 N.C.O's. and 16 O.Rs. from [illegible] Coy.

11 Transport Officer will arrange for the following :-
[illegible] FARM midnight half Limber per Coy. (Lewis Guns)
" 1 Limber H.Qrs. and 4 [illegible] under 2Lt. [illegible]
[illegible] FARM 10 p.m. Mess and Maltese carts.
[illegible] 1.30 a.m. O.C., Adjutant's. and Coy. Commanders horses.

12 Completion of relief will be wired to Bn. H.Qrs. by code word "[illegible]" - in billets will be reported by runner.

13 A C K N O W L E D G E.

(Sd.) [illegible] Capt. A/Adjutant
1st. Royal Munster Fusiliers.

Issued to:-

No. 1. Hd.Qrs. [illegible] Inf. Bde.	10. [illegible]
2. [illegible] Coy.	11 [illegible]
3. [illegible] Coy.	12 [illegible]
4. [illegible] Coy.	13. [illegible]
5. [illegible] Coy.	12 & 13 War Diary
6. [illegible]	14. File.
7. [illegible] Officer.	

SECRET.   OPERATION ORDERS No.21.   Copy No. /5
                           BY
LIEUT.COLONEL A.R.KNGE.D.S.O. O/cDG 1st R.MUNSTER FUSILIERS.
==

1. The Battalion will relieve the 2/7th Bn.K.O.S.L.R. in
   the Line on the night of the 22/23rd instant.

2. "X"Coy will relieve "B"Coy,K.O.S.L.R.   (Left Front).
   "Z" "   "   "   "C" "   "   (Right ").
   "Y" "   "   "   "D" "   "   (Support   ).
   "W" "   "   "   "A" "   "   (Reserve   ).

3. Coy Commanders will reconnoitre the Line tomorrow, leaving
   at 9.a.m.

4. The following Advance Parties will proceed to the Line
   on night 21/22nd instant. Report orderly Room- 9.p.m.-
   1.Officer per Coy. 1.Sergeant per Platoon. 1/Cpl Desmond
   and 2 Bn.H.Q. Runners. No's 1 and 3.Lewis Gun Teams.
   1. man for each of forward posts.
   Guides will be provided at rate of one per Coy,at 10-45.p.m.
   at Junction - Mule Track-with FONTAINEHAMEL - COUTURELLE -
   ROAD.(H.27.d.50.75).
   Lewis Gun Ammunition, with the exception of 12 drums per
   gun, will be taken by these parties.

5. On night of relief, guides at the rate of 1 per platoon
   will be at above Rendezvous (H.27.d.50.75) at 11.p.m.
   Coys will leave Camp at the following times :-
   "X" Coy - 9.p.m.   "Z"Coy - 9.15.p.m.   "Y"Coy - 9.20.p.m.
        "W" Coy - 9.25.p.m.   "Y.H" Coy - 9.30.p.m.
   Distances to be observed - 200 yards between Coys.
   100 yards between Platoons.
   ROUTE - via. ROSSIGNOL FARM - CHATEAU de la HAIE.

6. Great coats will be taken to Line. All men will carry
   120 rounds S.A.A. Lewis Gunners (50 rounds).

7. All Packs will be stacked outside Guard Room at 9.a.m.
   22nd instant.
   All tents and Billets will be cleaned up by 3.p.m.
   Certificates of cleanliness to be obtained from Advance
   Parties of incoming Unit.

8. All Defence Schemes, etc, and Trench Stores will be taken
   over. Copies of Reciepts to reach Bn.H.Q. by 10.a.m.23rd inst.

9. Transport Officer will arrange for following :-
   1 Limber for 6 Coys L.G.Ammunition,(para.4) Bn.H.q.6.p.m.
   21st instant.
   Removal of Packs (para.7).
   Bn.H.q. 9.p.m. 22nd - 2 Limbers,(L.G's).
     "   "   "   - Maltese Cart - Mess Cart.
     "   9.p.m. "   - Coy Commanders horses.

10. Completion of relief will be wired Bn.H.q.at once by
    Code Words - M.13.ENTED .

11. A C K N O W L E D G E.

                                   (Sd) C.V.HAR-DENS, Captain.
    21st JUNE,1915.   A/Adjutant,1st R.Munster Fusiliers.

Copies to - No.1. O.C.   No.7.O.C.2/7.K.O.S.L.R.
            2. H.q.172.I.Bde.   8.Sig. Officer.
            3. O.C. W Coy   9.T.O.& q.M.
            4. " X "   10.R.S.M.
            5. " Y "   11-12.War Diary.
            6. " Z "   13. Files.
            ....

1st Royal Munster Fusiliers

Page I

Army Form C. 2118.

WAR DIARY
or
INTELLIGENCE SUMMARY.
(Erase heading not required.)

Place	Date	Hour	Summary of Events and Information	Remarks and references to Appendices
COURCELETTE	1 July		Battalion & Company commanders of the 1st Bn Wellington Regt, New Zealand Division, came up to reconnoitre the line taken over & the dispositions. During the afternoon the enemy attempted to raid one of our advanced posts. Two of our men were killed & one wounded, but no prisoners taken on either side. Otherwise quiet.	
"	2nd		Bn relieved in the left sub-sector of the right sector by the 1st Wellington Regt. Two platoons of "A" Coy remained behind until relieved by the 1st Auckland Rifles tomorrow night. Bn proceeded to AUTHIE. Details from MARIEUX also rejoined the Bn at AUTHIE.	
AUTHIE	3rd		The day was spent settling down in camp & reorganising coys. All the officers & other ranks arranged under Major Nightingale reconnoitred the lost on & the RED LINE system allotted to the Bn to be held in the event of an enemy attack.	
"	4th		The Bn took part in a Bn tactical scheme which consisted of assembling in the RED LINE & manning the positions.	
AUTHIE	5th		The Bn carried out staff training from 9am to 1pm. Consisted of close order drill musketry & machine gun range & Bayonet tactical exercises. New organisation of platoons being composed of only 3 sections including 1 double section of Lewis Lyons teams, now adopted throughout the Bn.	
"	6th		Bn out training all the morning. Lt. Lt. Kane proceeds on leave & Major Nightingale took	

1st Royal Munster Fusiliers   Page 14

Army Form C. 2118.

WAR DIARY
or
INTELLIGENCE SUMMARY
(Erase heading not required.)

Place	Date	Hour	Summary of Events and Information	Remarks and references to Appendices
AUTHIE	13th July		Btn. received orders Bn. dispersed for classes.	
	14th		Bn. marched to B. SIEGER & took part in Bde. Sports.	
	15th		Btn. Coy. Serjeants Majors Night Ops. reconnoitred the Bois de WARNIMONT for a tactical Scheme in Attack.	
			Positions in RED LINE reconnoitred in the morning.	
	16-17th		Usual Training programme.	
	18th		Bn. carried out a tactical exercise in Bois de WARNIMONT in conjunction with Machine Gun Corps & a contact aeroplane.	
	20th		Usual Training in the morning. All Commanding Officers of Brigade reconnoitred new positions for assembly in later defence scheme, under Bde. G.O.C. Bde.	
	21st		Bn. marched to B. SIEGER & took part in Divisional Sports. Horse Shows.	
	22nd		Bn. out from 5.0 am. doing field Bn. tactical exercise. Demonstrated to WEGER for 2.30 pm 1st Half.	
	23rd		Bn. out at 4 am. for work on the PURPLE LINE system of trenches. Back by 11.30 am.	
	24th		Bn. always full took for two Days to carry the Divisional Commander, Capt. Hr.Bn getting best points in Horse Show.	
	25th		Be on cock the Bn. marched & some officers as the cross all the affairs.	
	26th		Practice for the Bn. tactical exercise in which the Bn. is representing the Enemy.	
	27th		Bn. paraded 6.30 am. took up their disposition for the tactical exercise cancelled on account of the rain.	

1st Royal Munster Fusiliers

Page IV

Army Form C. 2118.

WAR DIARY
or
INTELLIGENCE SUMMARY.
(Erase heading not required.)

Place	Date	Hour	Summary of Events and Information	Remarks and references to Appendices
AUTHIE	28		Received orders to move tomorrow early.	
SAULTY	29		Bn marched at 8.30am & marched to SAULTY where they were billetted & took one day's rest from travel.	
ETRUN	30		The Bn marched to ETRUN arriving in camp about 5pm.	
	1st		Commanding Officer & Coy Commanders proceed to ARRAS & thence to reconnoitre the support line in front.	
	2		The Bn proceeds to ARRAS at 8.30 p.m. to billets.	
	3			
	4			
	5			
	6			
	7			
	8			
	9			
	10			
	11			
	12			
	13			
	14			
	15			
	16			

1st Bn. Royal Munster Fus.
Daily Strength of Battn for month of July 1918.

DATE	STRENGTH	
	OFFRS.	O.Rs
July 1st	47	977
2	47	973
3	47	973
4	47	972
5	46	972
6	46	971
7	45	969
8	45	968
9	45	966
10	45	965
11	45	966
12	46	967
13	46	973
14	46	973
15	46	974
16	46	975
17	46	976
18	46	976
19	45	977
20	45	975
21	45	975
22	45	976
23	44	973
24	45	975
25	44	974
26	45	962
27	45	959
28	45	969
29	45	960
30	45	937
31	45	934

S E C R E T. OPERATION ORDERS No.22. COPY NR. 19
BY
LIEUT.COLONEL.R.R.KANE.DSO.COMDG.1st R.MUNSTER FUSILIERS.
==

less 3 Platoons "Y"Coy

1. The Battalion will be relieved by the 1st Bn.Wellington
   and the 1st Bn.Auckland on the night 1/2nd July as follows:-
   "T" Coy No's 1.2 & 4 Platoons will be relieved by "C"Coy
                                                    (Taranaki)1st Wellington
   "Y"Coy No.3 platoon will be relieved by "D"Coy(Machine)1st WELLINGTON
   "X" " No.7 & 8 Platoons   -do-   "D" "   -do-   -do-

   "Y" " No.5 & 6 Platoons   -do-   3rd "   1st Aucklands.
   "Y"Coy.No.10.Platoon.   -do-   "D" "   1st Wellington.
   "Z" " will be relieved by"B"Coy(Hawkes Bay) 1st Wellington.
   "H.Q"Coy will be relieved by H.Q.Coy 1st Auckland.
   "D"Coy will take over "X" Coy H.Q.
   "C" "   "   "   "   "Y" "   "
   "B" "   "   "   "   "Z" "   "
   "Y" " H.Q. will be taken over by 3rd.N.Z.Bde.

2. GUIDES. - Guides at the rate of 1 per platoon from No's
   1.2.3.4.7.8.10.13.14.15 & 16 Platoons will report to
   2/Lieut J.P.O'REILLY at Bn.H.Q.by 6.p.m . 1st July.They
   will meet platoons from 1st Wellington Regt at LONE TREE.
   (near Junction-BAILLY-PONQUEVILLERS-ROAD with MULE TRACK).
   and guide them to the Line at 10.p.m.
   Guides from No' 5 & 6 Platoons will report to 2/Lieut.
   O'REILLY at the same time and will guide Platoons from
   3rd Auckland Coy from Left Brigade at 10.p.m. to the Line.
   Guides for Posts will be at Coy H.Q.at 11.p.m.

3. On completion of relief 3 Platoons "Y"Coy (9.11.12) will
   come under the command of O.C.9th Bn.K.L.R.
   "Y"Coy will forward to Bn.H.Q.by noon July 1st,a complete
   List of Trench Stores.Ammunition ,Deep Dug-outs,etc, to
   be handed over by the 3 platoons.
   Rations for 2nd inst for these platoons will be put on
   Limbers of 9th Bn.K.L.R.(Please Notify quartermaster.Men
   to carry up these rations will be sent to H.Q. 9th Bn.
   K.L.R.(R.4.a.5.2) at 10.p.m.1st July.
   These Platoons when relieved on night 2/3rd will march
   out with their Lewis guns. 9th Bn.K.L.R. will provide
   Transport for same.

4. On completion of relief,Battalion will proceed via.
   PONQUEVILLERS-COURCOURT ROAD-MULE TRACK to BOYASTRE.No
   Companies will not pass PONQUEVILLERS-COURCOURT-ROAD
   till they are complete. Distances of 200 yards between
   Coys and 100 yards between platoons will be observed.
   Companies will embus under supervision of 2/Lieut O'Reilly
   at BOMA-SEME for LOUVENCOURT,when a hot meal will be ser-
   ved and billets obtained.(Quarter Master please note)
   Battalion will proceed to A U T H I E on 2nd July(after noon)
   at a time to be notified later. Camp will be taken over
   from 4th N.Z.R.B. at I.16.d.5.6.

5. Following Advance Parties will report to Quarter Master
   at COIGNEUX by 10.p.m.30th instant :-
   2/Lieut TEEHAN and 1 N.C.O.from each Coy. They will
   proceed to AUTHIE and take over camp from 4th Bn.N.Z.R.B.
   by 9.a.m . 1st JULY. Rations for 2nd will be carried.
   Advance Parties which proceeded to LOUVENCOURT this morning under 2/Lieut.O'Donnell will meet Companies on night
   1/2nd July and guide them to Billets.

6. 4 Lewis Guns per Coy and 8 drums per gun will proceed
   on Busses with the Battalion.
   The remainder will be stacked at Bn.H.Q.under care of
   Lewis Gun Officer and taken to Transport Lines.

7. (a) All Defence Schemes Programmes of Work, Maps and Aeroplane Photographs will be handed over.
   (b) Trench and area stores will be handed over.
   (c) Petrol Tins and Hot Food Containers (excluding Mobile Reserve) will be handed over.
   Separate receipts for (a)(b) &(c) will reach Bn.H.Q. by noon 3rd July.
   Detailed Lists of all ammunition and grenades (shewing description) handed over in their area will be sent to Bn. H.Q. by noon July 3rd.

8. Surplus personnel at MARIEUX will report to Adjutant at AUTHIE on after noon July 2nd. They will be in charge of Captain. CALWELL.M.C.

9. All areas occupied by the Bn. will be left scrupulously clean. Certificates for same from all Companies, Transport Officer and Quartermaster will reach Bn.H.Q. by noon 3rd JULY.

10. Transport Lines will be taken over on 2nd July at X.16.c.9.6. from 1st Otagos.
    Advance parties will take ove on July 1st by 9.a.m.
    Baggage Wagons will report at Transport Lines 9.a.m. July 2nd. Two trips may be made and they will then return to No.4 Coy Divisional Train.
    1 Motor Lorry will report Divisional Reception Camp at 12 noon July 2nd, to move Details, Kit, etc, to AUTHIE. Loading and unloading parties will be provided from DETAILS, also Guides.
    Following Transport will be required on night of relief (para.6) :- By arrangement with Lewis Gun Officer -
    Mess Cart Bn.H.Q. 11.p.m. also 1 Limber per Coy.

11. Completion of relief will be wired Bn.H.Q. by Code Words - M.51.NOTED.
    Arrival in Billets LOUVENCOURT will be reported by runner.

12. A C K N O W L E D G E.

Issued at 9.p.m. 30th inst.
                                    (Sd) C.W. MARSDEN, Captain,
JUNE 30th 1918.   A/Adjutant, 1st R.Munster Fusiliers.

ISSUED TO :-
        No.1. H.Q.172 Inf.Bde.
        2. H.Q.3rd N.Z.Bde.
        3. O.C.1st Wellington.
        4. O.C.1st Auckland.
        5. O.C.9th Bn. K.L.R.
        6-9-O.C.W.X.Y.Z.Coys.
        10.R.S.M.
        11.Int. Officer.
        12. Qr-Mr & T.O.
        13. Lewis Gun Officer.
        14.Adjutant(DETAILS)
        15-16-War Diary.
        17-18.Spare.
        19.File.

SECRET   4022   Copy No. 12

OPERATION ORDERS
By
Major G. W. NIGHTINGALE M.C. Comdg. 1st. Royal Munster Fusiliers.
In the Field 15. 7. 18

****

Ref. Map 57d.N.W. 1/20,000 Corrected to 9. 5. 18.

INFORMATION

(a) The enemy are reported to be in the villages of COIGNEUX, BUS-LES-ARTOIS and LOUVENCOURT and are strongly entrenched in a system of trenches running through the Eastern edge of the BOIS-DE-WARNIMONT covering the village of BUS-LES-ARTOIS.

(b) Our troops are in AUTHIE and VAUCHELLES with advanced posts in the BOIS DE WARNIMONT in touch with the enemy.

INTENTION.

The Battalion will take part in a Brigade attack on the morning of the 18th;inst; Battalion Final objective - Enemy's entrenched position from I.24.b.75 to I.24.d.01. and the first objective will be from I.24.b.48. to I.24.c.84.
It is assumed that the 2/4th.South.Lancs. will be co-operating on the right and the 9th. Kings Liverpool Regiment on the left.

INSTRUCTIONS.

(a) The Battalion will assemble for the attack in the dead ground North of the AUTHIE - BUS LES ARTOIS road at I.23.b.76. and will form up in three lines.
    1. Front Line (for first objective) W.Coy.
    2. Second Line (for final objective) Y.Coy. on Rt.
        "   "   "   "   "   X.Coy. on Lt.
    3. Reserve .... Z.Coy.

(b) W.Coy. will advance on a front covering whole of first objective, with one platoon south of the AUTHIE-BUS LES ARTOIS road and three platoons north of the same road.
X and Y Coys. will follow W Coy. after interval of ten minutes, and will pass through it and take the final objective.
Y Coy. will operate South of the AUTHIE - BUS LES ARTOIS road and X Coy. north of the road.

(c) Z.Coy will remain at the assembly point until it receives instructions from Battalion H.Qrs.

(d) A detachment from the 57th. Divisional Machine Gun Corps will co-operate on the flanks.

(e) Time of attack - The attacking force will leave the assembly point at 11-0 a.m.

LIAISON.

A contact aeroplane will co-operate in the attack and maintain communication between the attacking troops and Battalion H.Qrs.
For this purpose flares will be lit by W.Coy. at approximately 11-30 a.m. and at any time when called for by the aeroplane, the signal being a succession of A's on Klazon horn and a White Very Light. Similarly Y and X Coys. will make known their position at 12-0 noon, when they should have reached their objective.

S.A.A.

Ammunition Pack Animals will concentrate at point I.23.b.76. and come under the orders of the R.S.M.

AID POST.

At I.18.a.10.

REPORTS

Report centre at point I.18.a.10.

                 (Sd.) C.W.MARSDEN.   Captain
                 Adjutant 1st.Royal Munster Fusiliers.

Issued at :-

Copy No. 1   W.Coy
         2   X.Coy
         3   Y.Coy
         4   Z.Coy
         5   59th. Squadron R.A.F. (Doullens)
         6   57th. M.G.C.
         7   172nd. Infantry Brigade
         8   Commanding Officer
         9 to 12   War Diary and File.

OPERATION ORDERS

BY

Major G.W.NIGHTINGALE MC. Comdg. 1st.Batt. The Roy.Munster Fus.
In the Field. 25/7/18.

Ref.Map 57D. N.W. 1/20,000
do. 57D. 1/40,000

1. INFORMATION. The Batt; will take part in a Brigade Tactical Exercise, on Saturday, and will provide the enemy.
The 172nd.Brigade less this Batt; will attack the position - the 2/4th.S.Lancs:Regt: on the right and the 9th.K.L.R. on the left. The following will be the dispositions of the Batt; in the defence.

2. DISPOSITIONS.
(1) W.Coy, with one platoon from X Coy. and one platoon from Y Coy. will hold an outpost line from I.27.a.6.2. to I.21.d.8.7, all six platoons in the line forming a series of strong points, on the all round defence system.
(2) X and Y Coys. less one platoon will form the Main Line of resistance 100 yards East of the AUTHIE-VAUCHELLES Road. X Coy. will be on the left and Y Coy. on the right. Boundaries as decided on previously by Coy. Commanders.
(3) Z Coy. will be in Reserve and will be used as Counter-attack Coy. The formation for the counter-attack will be on a two platoon frontage in two waves of two platoons.
(4) A party of one officer and 40 other ranks (10 from each Coy.) will represent the Artillery Barrage.

3. DRESS. Battle Order.

4. AMMUNITION. Pack mules with reserve ammunition will remain in the Sunken Road in I.28.b. and come under the orders of the R.S.M.

5. COMMUNICATION. By visual and runners between Coys. and Bn.H.Q.

6. REPORTS. Report centre will be at Bn.H.Q. at the junction of the tracks at I.28.a.3.5.

7. BATT:O.P. A Batt; O.P.will be established on top of the Ridge about I.28.c.8.3.

8. SYNCHRONIZATION. Watches will be synchronized at Bn.H.Q. one hour before Zero. Zero hour for scheme will probably be 3-0p.m. for the attacking troops.

(Sd.) C.W.MARSDEN. Capt:& Adjt;
1st.Bn.The Royal Munster Fusiliers

OPERATION ORDERS.

by

Major C.W.[illegible] M.C. Comdg. 1st.Btn. Royal [illegible] Fus.
In the Field. [illegible].7.18

---

1. The Battalion will move to [illegible] to-morrow the [illegible] inst. Parade on Battalion parade ground ready to move off at [illegible].
Dress :- Full marching order . Steel helmets will be worn.

2. Capt. [illegible] M.C. will act as second in command , riding in rear of the Battalion , and be responsible that stragglers are collected in parties, and that they march into their new billeting areas in their own time.

3. All huts , Defence Schemes, etc; will be handed over to [illegible] to-morrow morning . All trench stores and camp dumps will be handed over .
Receipts for same will be sent to Battn.H.Q. ([illegible]) by 6-0p.m.
Capt.[illegible] MC will stay behind and hand over the Camp.
Advance Parties, from [illegible] will arrive at [illegible] to-morrow.

4. Advance Parties. One Corporal per Coy. and 2/Lt. [illegible] will report at Orderly Room to [illegible] at 9-30 a.m.
They will proceed on bicycles to [illegible] and report to Town Major at 10-30 a.m. and arrange for billeting the Battalion. N.C.O's. from this party will be sent to the X roads south of [illegible] at 12-30p.m. to guide their Coys. to billets.

5. All kits will be stacked at Q.M's. stores by [illegible].
Baggage Wagons will march with the Bttn.
Motor Lorry for the Battalion will report at the Brigade H.Q. [illegible] at [illegible]. The Q.M. will send a guide for the lorry at this time.

6. The following March Discipline will be strictly adhered to. -;
The Battalion Intelligence Officer and 6 Scouts will lead the Battalion. Intelligence Officer will synchronise watches with the Brigade Signalling Officer at the starting point (Cross Roads [illegible]) at 10-30 a.m. [illegible] will drop guides at Cross Roads etc.
Each Coy. will have one Lewis Gun Limber and the Cooker in rear of the Coy. The remainder of the Transport will be in the rear of the Battn. under Transport Officer. 100 Yards interval between Coys. and 100 yards interval between the Transport, and the Battn.
Ten minutes halt at ~~[illegible]~~ ten minutes to each clock hour.

7. Coys. will report to Battn. H.Q. as soon as they are complete in billets.

8. Acknowledge.

(Sd.) [illegible] Capt. & Adjt.
1st.Bn. Royal [illegible] Fus.

OPERATION ORDERS

BY

Lt.Col. R.R.G.KANE DSO. Comdg. 1st.Bn. Royal Munster Fus.
in the Field. 31.7.18

1. The Battalion will move to billets at ARRAS to-night.
   Parade behind H.Q.Hut ready to move off at 7-15p.m.
   Dress:- Full marching order, steel helmets will be worn.

2. Following Advance parties will report at Orderly Room
   at 6-0p.m. to-night
       One Officer per Coy.
       One N.C.O. from each platoon,
       One do. Headquarter Coy.
       Two representatives from each Lewis Gun Sec.
       (each representative will carry 8 L.G.drums)
       One officer from W.Coy. to take over dumps.
       Senior officer will report to Adjt. at 5-30p.m.
   Lorries will take this party as far as possible and they
   will proceed then to the crater ARRAS — BAILLEUL road
   G.12.a.3.7. where guides from CANADIANS will be at
   9-15p.m.

3. T.O. will arrange for Transport of Lewis Guns to ARRAS
   with the Battn. All L.G's to go to line will be at
   Transport Lines by 6-0p.m.
   Mess Cart will move with Battn. also Limbers with rations.

4. Transport Lines and Q.M.Stores will remain in present
   position.

5. Surplus Personnel and Orderly Room Staff will proceed
   to AISNE CAMP to-night.
   Parade 5-0p.m. Officer's Kits will be stacked at Q.M.
   Stores by 4-0p.m. Transport Officer will arrange
   Transport.

6. During period Batt. is in ARRAS there must be no
   movement by day.

7. Distances on march as yesterday. Dixies will be taken
   into line. Water supply in ARRAS is adequate (T.O.Note)

8. Coy.Commanders will report complete in Billets in
   ARRAS as soon as possible to Batt.H.Q.

9. Acknowledge.

Issued to.
    W.X.Y.Z. Coys.
    T.O. & Q.M.
    2nd. in Com.
    R.S.M.
    2 War Diary. (Sd.) C.W.MARSDEN Capt. & Adjt.
    H.Q.#72 Bde.   for 1st.Batt. Roy.Munster Fus.

1st Royal Newcastle Fusiliers

WAR DIARY
or
INTELLIGENCE SUMMARY.
(Erase heading not required.)

Army Form C. 2118.
Page I

Vol 30

Place	Date	Hour	Summary of Events and Information	Remarks and references to Appendices
ETRUN	August 1918	7PM	The Battalion less surplus personnel marched to ARRAS and billeted in the town preparatory to going into the front line. Surplus personnel proceeded to the 5/Division Reception Camp at ASHES LES DUISANS	
ARRAS	2.8.18		The Battalion proceeded to the Support position of the Bn. behind TAMPOUX. Coy HQrs were established in the railway cutting near ATHIES. Rear Bn. HQrs in ARRAS.	
ATHIES	2-8 to 8-8-18		Bn. remained in same position, but sent 1 coy. up into the front line N. of TAMPOUX. Very quiet part of the line - two casualties.	
WAKEFIELD CAMP	9.8.18		The Bn. moved to WAKEFIELD Camp S. of ROCLINCOURT leaving 1 company WEST of ATHIES.	

1st Royal Munster Fusiliers.   Part II

Army Form C. 2118.

WAR DIARY
or
INTELLIGENCE SUMMARY.
(Erase heading not required.)

Instructions regarding War Diaries and Intelligence Summaries are contained in F. S. Regs., Part II. and the Staff Manual respectively. Title pages will be prepared in manuscript.

Place	Date	Hour	Summary of Events and Information	Remarks and references to Appendices
WAKEFIELD CAMP	10		Brigade & Coy in MUSKETRY Vickery firing marking pointers.	
	11		C.O.'s Parade. Sports etc.	
	12		do	Applications ranges
	13		do	
	14		do	
	15		Inspection for musketry into the Field Courses Hazebrouck X Coy	
	16		Inspected Platoon training. Officers attended demonstration B Coy musketry at HEDIGN EVL.	
	17	1600	Inspected Platoon training.	
			7th BLACK WATCH to-do hand & north Bn.	
FREMICOURT	18	0600	East and Artillery Group (20th Ky) Relieved CHILDERS Group 6 FUSILIERS.	
	19		Training.	
	20		Training - bay schemes on Road from near CHERIE	
	21		Training - Officers and NCOs to lecture at TINCQUES - Lecture Infantry escorts tanks in the attack.	

1st Royal Munster Fusiliers   Part III

WAR DIARY
or
INTELLIGENCE SUMMARY.
(Erase heading not required.)

Army Form C. 2118.

Ref. FRANCE / sheet 51/SW

Place	Date May	Hour	Summary of Events and Information	Remarks and references to Appendices
NOYELLE REMY	22		Marched midnight 21/22 from FAVREUIL to NOYELLE REMY & billeted therein	
GROUCHES	23		Marched midnight 22/23 to GROUCHES arriving 0600 - billeted	
BAVINCOURT	24		Marched midnight 23/24 to BAVINCOURT - billeted	
RONSART	25		Marched midday to RONSART & bivouacked	
	26		Marched midnight 26/27 to FICHEUX	
FICHEUX	27		Arrived 0600 & occupied reserve trenches. Bn did later area HENIN & to of to perform in HINDENBURG SUPPORT. 2 Coy about TC b 2,3 W " " U 1 a 5,8 X " " T 6 a 5,6 Y " " O 31 c 1,3 HQ at T 56 52	

1st Royal Munster Fusiliers   Part II

Army Form C. 2118.

WAR DIARY
or
INTELLIGENCE SUMMARY.
(Erase heading not required.)

Instructions regarding War Diaries and Intelligence
Summaries are contained in F. S. Regs., Part II.
and the Staff Manual respectively. Title pages
will be prepared in manuscript.

Place	Date	Hour	Summary of Events and Information	Remarks and references to Appendices
HEMINEL	28/27 Sept 1918		Brigade the right of Line 27/28 Fus. Assembled in a sunken behind RIENCOURT HENDICOURT in support position to the 2nd Irish Guards Bord Regt & 2/4th Leinster Regt.	
		12.42 P.M	The Battalion after 9 hrs 40 mins today advanced 2m to support & was on the left.	
		1 PM	Battalion supported by advance.	
		1.15 PM	The Battalion came under considerable Machine gun fire from the CROISILLES – FONTAINE road, but the line moved steadily. established about BOVIS LANE – FAG ALLEY – the front objective	
		3 PM	The enemy appears beaten by a considerable extent, but 2 coys had moved toward Regt. Support from the shoulder of the sunken road. We did not identify.	
		5.45 PM	Orders were received from Brigade that we & 3/4 Y Coy were to take up the FAG ALLEY.	
MARTIN SUR	29 Sept 1918		Orders received from 2nd Bde H.Q. to send back the Bn. to be transported into the valley and to attack by 5.30pm ST MARTIN SUR COJEUL.	
COJEUL		6 P.M	The Bn took up position in the HINDENBURG LINE, E. of the village of ST MARTIN SUR COJEUL.	
	30 Sept		Remained in same position & reorganized.	
	31st A.M		Remained as in the previous days.	

Sgd. M.S. MacMurray Major
pr R Munster Fusiliers

OFFICER'S CASUALTIES.

```
Capt. C.H. Carrigan.M.C  Killed in Action.      2-9-18.
2/Lieut. S.P. Carson.           do.             2-9-18.
2/Lieut. A.L. McFarlane. Died from wounds.      2-9-18.
2/Lieut. F.G. O'Donnell. Wounded.              30-8-18.
2/Lieut. J. McLoughlin.         do.             2-9-18.
2/Lieut. J.L. Doherty.          do.             2-9-18.
2/Lieut. M.P. Feehan.           do.             2-9-18.
Lieut. E.J. Mahony.      Killed in Action.     27-9-18.
2/Lieut. W.P. Gore.             do.            27-9-18.
2/Lieut. H.R. McCormack. Wounded.              27-9-18.
Capt. W.T. Caldwell. M.C.       do.            28-9-18.
2/Lieut. E.H. Tyler.            do.            29-9-18.
Lt. Col. R.R. Kane. D.S.O.      do.            30-9-18.
                         Died from wounds.
Capt. T.H. Poingdestre.  Wounded.              30-9-18.
Lieut. M.H. Fitzgerald. M.C.    do.            30-9-18.
Lieut. M. Nunan.                do.            30-9-18.
2/Lieut. E.G.S. Dannagher.      do.            30-9-18.
2/Lieut. F.J. Maybury.          do.            30-9-18.
```

Honours gained during the month of Sept. 1918.

MILITARY CROSS.

2/Lieut. J.P. May. M.M.

2/Lieut. C. J. Bergin.

2/Lieut. J.P. O'Reilly.

DISTINGUISHED CONDUCT MEDAL.

814. Sgt. Amos. J.

7538. Sgt. Costigan. W.

MILITARY MEDAL.

4101. Pte. Doran. M.
9437. Sgt. Noonan. J. D.C.M.
18062. Pte. Wilson. R.
15138. Sgt. Alford. T.
7526. Cpl. Frawley. J.
18272. Pte. Malin. T.
5855. Pte. Pettifer. J.
7195. Pte. Kelly. T.
7819. Pte. O'Connor. C.
18304. Pte. Nolan. E.
5545. Pte. Scully. S.
6763. Pte. Cambridge. D.
8859. Pte. Merner. J.

APPENDIX. L.I (c)

Report on Operations of August 28th 1918

The Battalion formed up ready to attack by 12 noon.

The attack was made on a two Company frontage, each Company being on a two platoon frontage.

B Company (Captain R.B Fairclough) attacked on the right; A Company (Lieut. H.G Bullen) on the left; C Company (Lieut. C.W Hodson) followed B Company, and D Company (Captain L.J McLuno M.C) followed A Company.

On reaching the first objective C and D Companies were to leap frog through and capture the second objective.

The Barrage of the Divisions on either flank fell some minutes before our own. The leading Companies however began to move forward without waiting for our barrage.

The enemy put down his barrage very quickly on the forward edge of and in the village of Fontaine.

Several casualties were caused here, amongst them being Lieut. H.G Bullen, who however continued to command his Company until the evening.

The advance progressed very well, the men going forward splendidly.

check until reaching the first objective where we began to check them under heavy machine gun fire from the left bank. Lieut. Hodson was wounded in getting through the wire.

C and D Companies entered the village of Hendicourt and got as far as the Central Road but heavy Machine Gun fire from the left and left rear, and the fact that the Division on our left had been held up, leaving our flank exposed, caused Captain D. J. Mearns M.C. to withdraw these Companies to line of our first objective.

Parties of the 9th Bn Kings entered the same village on the right flank. These parties also withdrew on to the line of our first objective.

Captain D. J. Mearns M.C. consolidated his position in Cemetery Avenue (our first objective) while Captain R B Fairclough threw out a defensive outpost line towards the right rear, as there appeared to be a gap at this point.

These were the positions which were held during the night.

At dawn the Battalion was relieved by the 170th Infantry Brigade and withdrew into reserve.

Our casualties were

- 3 -

five officers wounded, one officer missing and 200 other ranks killed, wounded and missing. Some of these men are expected to rejoin shortly.

The following officers did particularly well:-

Captain D. J. Mearns M.C. who maintained his position and organised the defence of it with his left flank and left rear exposed;

Lieut. A. G. Bullen, who although wounded and severely shaken by shell fire at the commencement of the advance, continued on duty until the evening.

Lieut G. S. Lambert, M.O.R.C. U.S.A, who worked unceasingly from 1-30 pm until 8-30 pm, being under shell fire for some considerable period.

The following points were noticeable as requiring improvement;-

(1). The means of obtaining information as to the general situation.

(2). The maintenance of communication between Battalions and Brigades.

(3). The provision of stretchers and bearers by A.D.S.

In the first case it is suggested that one or more officers or reliable N.C.O. should always be employed

- 4 -

to keep in touch with the situation and report to the Commanding Officer as has been previously laid down by the G.O.C, but which was not done on this occasion.

Regarding the second point, the detailing of an officer to carry orders between Brigade and Battalions was very usefully employed in the earlier stages, and would have been of great assistance in getting through orders quickly if it had been continued to the end of the operations. Also the ~~advanced~~ Advanced Brigade Report Centre was not sufficiently made use of.

Regarding the third point, on this occasion the Battalion was not able to get in touch with the A.D.S. sufficiently early, and in consequence had to do most of the carrying to A.D.S, as well as from the front line to R.A.P. There was also a considerable shortage of stretchers, and wounded had to be left at the R.A.P for long periods before being removed to A.D.S.

It is suggested that as the R.A.P is always in close touch with B.H.Q that the Brigade should inform the Medical Services of the position of Battalion Headquarters as

-5-

soon as the location report is
received from Battalions.

J.H.Monkhouse(?)
Lieut-Colonel
Commanding
29-8-18.   2/4th Bn South Lancashire Regt

1st Royal Munster Fusiliers

Page 1
1 R Munsters
Army Form C. 2118.
September 1918.

WAR DIARY or INTELLIGENCE SUMMARY.
(Erase heading not required.)

Instructions regarding War Diaries and Intelligence Summaries are contained in F.S. Regs., Part II. and the Staff Manual respectively. Title pages will be prepared in manuscript.

Place	Date	Hour	Summary of Events and Information	Remarks and references to Appendices
TUNNEL TRENCH (N. of FONTAINE LES CROISILLES)	Sept 1st	9 AM	Bn. remained in TUNNEL TRENCH all day. Reorganised & waited for 9 PM. Orders were received for the attack on the following day.	
	2nd	2 PM	H.Q. moved to a system of trenches W. of HENDICOURT.	
		4.48	H.Q.B. "moved up". Zero hour, but the troops did not start until 5 AM. look at the position on the objective.	
DROCOURT-QUEANT Switch, due E. of RIENCOURT		6 PM	2000 hours & the tanks returned to the operation, 5 in number. The objectives in the DROCOURT-QUEANT Switch were reached & consolidated. Result was un- satisfactory. There being no counter-attack by the enemy.	
TUNNEL TRENCH	3rd	2 PM	H.Q. Bn. were relieved by the DROCOURT-QUEANT line & proceeded to Tunnel Trench B. Green CROISILLES.	
ADINFER	4,5,6		For these days the Bn. remained in the Sunken Road, reorganising & refitting 2nd Battle Supplies, personnel from HENDECOURT before the Bn. on this. A reconnaissance of the Sector between COURCOURT and QUEANT was made on the 5th afternoon by the 86th.	
	7th	1 AM	The Bn. proceeded to Trenches known as QUEER STREET N. of PRONVILLE, in support to the front line at NOEUVRES. The B.G. was then in support to the division.	
	8th-14th		The Bn. was taken over from the ANZAC Bn. of the 63rd Naval Division, and was in support until the 1st series, reserve resources were carried out & a Queen Scheme comprising a counter-attack on NOEUVRES was planned.	
NOEUVRES	14th/15th /15th	Night	Bn. Rel. 11 R. St? ? (Rifles?) in the front line sector N. of NOEUVRES. The enemy heavily occupied NOEUVRES on this day previous to this. Patrols pushed out on the line, 2 coys re-established all the posts of our additional. Pushed a line East to CEMETERY TRENCH leading towards the CANAL BANK. Enemy artillery very active all day. Heavy sniping & artillery Scout shelling. Trs.B? behind the night Sub-Sector by the Bn. on the right.	

(A10266) Wt. W5909/P273 750,000 2/18 Sch. 52 Forms/C2118/16
D. D. & L., London, E.C.

1st Royal Munster Fusiliers

PAGE II

WAR DIARY or INTELLIGENCE SUMMARY

Army Form C. 2118

(Erase heading not required.)

Instructions regarding War Diaries and Intelligence Summaries are contained in F. S. Regs., Part II. and the Staff Manual respectively. Title pages will be prepared in manuscript.

Place	Date	Hour	Summary of Events and Information	Remarks and references to Appendices
MOEUVRES	14.9.18		Except for shelling, nothing of importance to record. Sev. prisoners & 1st Pruss. Gds. were taken.	
"	15.9		2 Coy. Baty. took over a part of the order of the Brigade on our right flank. Owing to night En.	
			mons. attacks on our lines EASTERLY posts, but were driven off. Several occasions to our lines S.	
			MONDAY again attacked the post without success. Mounted a barrage a prepared to patrol in the	
		4 A.M	day. After a short preliminary bombardment a platoon of 2 Coy attacked & recaptured the post captured by	
			the enemy during the night & established two block positions E of captured line. Enemy headless prisoners	(ISN)
BULLECOURT WEST	20/1/5		Bn. reserve & bivouaced in huts at Q.6.a.1.2. S.4 of the 33rd Division. Proceeded to the wagon lines.	(ISN)
BAILLEULMONT	17th		At BULLECOURT.	BAILLEULMONT
	18.9—29		Bn. proceeded to BOYELLES, where it entrained for BAUMETZ, marched from thence to BAILLEULMONT	(ISN)
			Reinforcements in billets at BAILLEULMONT. Prepared attack rehearses manoeuvres.	
LAGNICOURT	24.9	9.30	Bn. marched to BAUMETZ & thence by railway to VADIX—VAUCOURT, marched thence to LAGNICOURT via	(ISN)
		a.m	MERCATEL & BOIURLON. forming reserve Batt. Staying at BOYELLES	
			Bn. Bivouaced at LAGNICOURT until Day.	
"	26.9		Bn. marched to assembly trenches E of PRONVILLE	
	27th	2 P.M	Bn. to TADPOLE COPSE & formed up ready for the attack.	
		5.20 a.m	Bn. attack proceeded in front of the Br Bn & meanwhile the way across the Canal du Nord & captured & Officers 31 men & 1 M.G.	
			few German stuff handed in & took M57. The Bn crossed & thus took a heavy machine artillery fire about between GRAINCOURT.	

1st Bn Manchester Regiment

Page III

Army Form C. 2118.

WAR DIARY or INTELLIGENCE SUMMARY
(Erase heading not required.)

Place	Date	Hour	Summary of Events and Information	Remarks and references to Appendices
CANTAING	27/9/18	11 A.M.	The Bn. moved across the open ground about 300 yards systematically held up by heavy M.G. [machine gun] fire and CANTAING Village. Posts of machine gun fire opened up from own artillery barrage which held back the supporting Battns. on their way to open a flank on the village. Visitors received about 11 am. Moved the word of operation having been made with the artillery, a barrage was put down in the morning of the Bn. & parts of village of CANTAING & troops of another Bn. had through them. The Bn. remained in CANTAING village.	(over)
	28/9/18		News was received that the Bn. was to proceed from CANTAING to follow any reopened from the outskirts of CAMBRAI.	(over)
	29/9/18	11.30am	The Bn. moved forward, crossed the ST QUENTIN CANAL & moved in artillery formation towards the village of PROVILLE.	(over)
PROVILLE		12 noon	Held up by machine gun fire from the direction of PROVILLE. With the help of our artillery barrage the Bn. was able to move forward & took up a line opposite PROVILLE, on the outskirts of CAMBRAI. After the operation the Bn. received orders to reorganise. Some detached parties of the 2/Scot Rams D.S.O. was mortally wounded whilst engaged to reorganise for fresh attack.	(over)
		4pm.	Orders to Flying Counter-attack. A post was put out. O.S.M. was taken prisoner, but while the Bn was of the Green Bn of the 3rd Naval Division. This post was retaken at 5pm.	(over)
		6pm.	The advanced troops were withdrawn, & a line taken up, just in rear of this position. Names held by the Bn throughout the night reduced to K.15.170–284.	(over)

W.H. McCullough Major
Actg Lt-Colonel Commanding
1st Battn Manchester Regiment

WAR DIARY or INTELLIGENCE SUMMARY

1st Battalion The Royal Munster Fusiliers

Page I

Place	Date	Hour	Summary of Events and Information	Remarks and references to Appendices
LA FOLIE WOOD	Oct 1st 1918 to Oct 4th		N.Bn. remained in LA FOLIE WOOD, reorganizing & resting. Bn. HQrs. in a sunken road & the companies in trenches in the wood. Slight shelling, but very few casualties. On the night of the 4th/5th Oct. the Bn. moved forward slightly. 2 coys. went into a support position E. of the ST QUENTIN CANAL. N. remained in practice/same place, about 1500 yards further into the wood.	
"	5.6. 1918		Bn. received orders to go into the front line trenches round the outskirts of CAMBRAI, the Bn. in support. Heavy shelling & considerable machine gun fire (in trenches on PROVILLE)	
PROVILLE	6th	3AM	The Bn. was ordered to clear up the situation with regard to a doubtful position to the enemy. 2 coys. were detailed to carry out the operation, which were shortly successful, the advance being captured & many of the enemy Killed & the rest put to flight.	
"	7th am		The Bn. remained in the same position on the night of 7th/8th. They were a heavy gas shelling by the enemy. Few casualties. Bn. HQrs. at the N. West PROVILLE. In the morning we prepared our forward line the 8th Aug. At dawn the coys attempted to enter a clump opposite our front trench ... never were received from B.H. to push forward patrols into CAMBRAI. At 9am two companies moved forward with the intent of progress certain situations. At 9am. Bn. HQ established in a house on the railway.	
ANNEUX	7th	7PM	Bn. received orders to proceed by road to BOURSIES & bivouac for the night. Bn. marched from ANNEUX to BOURSIES & bivouacked for the night in HINDENBORG LINE.	
ANNEUX	10th			

1st Royal Munster Fusiliers

Army Form C. 2118.

Page II

WAR DIARY
or
INTELLIGENCE SUMMARY.

(Erase heading not required.)

Instructions regarding War Diaries and Intelligence Summaries are contained in F. S. Regs., Part II. and the Staff Manual respectively. Title pages will be prepared in manuscript.

Place	Date	Hour	Summary of Events and Information	Remarks and references to Appendices
BOURSIES	11th Feb 1918		Lt. Col. E. C. LLOYD, D.S.O. Royal Irish Regt. took over command of the Bn. on instructions from B.H.Q. Bn. Rd. remained in camp all day.	
HERMIES	12th	3 P.M.	Bn. marched to HERMIES where it entrained for BETHUNE (qqv)	
BETHUNE	13th	0.30 A.M.	The Bn. arrived at BETHUNE & entrained. Marched to billets at VAUDRICOURT (5 kilos) qqv	
VAUDRICOURT	"	4 P.M.	Bn. billets in VAUDRICOURT. Orders received to be in readiness to move tomorrow A.M.	
"	14th	9 A.M.	Bn. marched to VERQUIN where it en-bused. The Bn. proceeded in buses to PONT du HEM on the road from BETHUNE – LA BASSEE road, & marched from there to LA TOUQUET arriving at 5 P.M. (qqv)	
LA TOUQUET	15th	6 A.M.	Bn. in support to Bns. in front line, the 47th Division being relieved by the 57th Division now to move forward. The relief to take place tonight was cancelled.	
"	"	9 A.M.	Information received that the enemy was retiring & the Bn. was at four hours notice to move forward.	
RADDINGHAM	16th	10 A.M.	Bn. still in same location. BR RADDINGHAM move forward. Orders received now at noon Bn. ordered to move.	
FIN DE LA GUERRE	17th	3 A.M.	Bn. Lt. RADDINGHAM & relieving the 9th Devon Regt. in the front line system of FIN DE LA GUERRE.	
SERQUE DIN	"	8 A.M.	Strong patrols reported no enemy resistance. Bn. moved forward & captured SERQUE DIN without opposition.	

1st Rhine water Division Page III

Army Form C. 2118.

WAR DIARY
or
INTELLIGENCE SUMMARY.
(Erase heading not required.)

Instructions regarding War Diaries and Intelligence Summaries are contained in F. S. Regs., Part II. and the Staff Manual respectively. Title pages will be prepared in manuscript.

Place	Date	Hour	Summary of Events and Information	Remarks and references to Appendices
SEQUEDIN	18/10/18		Bn remained at SEQUEDIN during the day & night.	
"	19th	12 noon	Bn marched to LE MARAIS & were billeted in that area (just west of LILLE)	
LE MARAIS	20th		Reorganisation & preparation of billets. Orders were received for the Bn to find a Guard of Honour for Monsieur POINCARÉ the President of France, who was visiting LILLE on the 21st. Parade state 17 officers 583 O.R.s	
"	"	6 AM	Orders received for the Bn to proceed tomorrow to ASCQ by a route passing through LILLE &c.	
LILLE	21st	6 AM	Bn marched off at 6am forward and started past Pont du CANTALEU at 7am. Marched through the city & out at the PONT DU LOUIS XIV & then proceeded to ASCQ arriving at 11.30 am.	
ASCQ	"	4 PM	Bn billeted for the night in ASCQ	
"		9 PM	Bn marched to WILLEMS & were billeted there	
WILLEMS	22.23.24		Bn remained in WILLEMS until the afternoon of the 24th Oct when it moved to CORNET. Took over the dispositions of the Reserve Bn in the Right Half Sector in the line. Bn had	
CORNET	25.26.27		in HARDY-PLANCK FARM, remainder of coys in billets in the village. Bn remained in Bn reserve. Nothing to report. Bn was relieved the 24.10.18 & proceeded to WILLEMS.	
HONNEVAIN	28th		Bn moved up into Bn Support at HONNEVAIN. Disposition of Coys. was "A" Coy in outpost position around TROYENNES (now billeted in house "B" Coy) "B" coy in Support in the village of HONNEVAIN. "W" Company in reserve. Bn H.Q. also in HONNEVAIN village.	

1st Royal Munster Fusiliers Page III

Army Form C. 2118.

WAR DIARY
or
INTELLIGENCE SUMMARY.

(Erase heading not required.)

Place	Date	Hour	Summary of Events and Information	Remarks and references to Appendices
HONNEVAIN	29th Oct		Bn. remained in same position. Posts & trenches dug & wire fixed & more guns placed in com- manding positions intermittent shelling during the canonnade.	
"	30th		Advance parties R.E. & 17th London Regt. arrived up to reconnoitre for positions. Orders received from Bde that the Bn. would be relieved on the 31st & proceed to AUSTAING. Considerable shelling during the night	
"	31st	7pm	Advanced billeting parties proceeded to AUSTAING & Fives	
		5pm	Relief completed & Bn. proceeded to AUSTAING arriving at 9PM. Three billets there & the night spent	

A. McIntyre Major
1st R.Munster Fusiliers

1st Bn. Royal Munster Fusiliers.

Officer Casualties for the Month of October 1918.

Lieut. Col. R.R. Kane. D.S.O.	Died from Wounds 1-10-18
2/Lieut. F.C. Mannox.	Wounded 6-10-18.
Lieut. M.H. Fitzgerald. M.C.	Inv. to U.K. 3-10-18. Wounded.
Lieut. G.H. Annaheim.	Killed in Action 4-10-18.
Lieut. H.E.V. Farrell.	Inv. to U.K. 1-10-18. Sick.
Lieut. M. Nunan.	Inv. to U.K. 3-10-18. Wounded.
2/Lieut. E.W. Tyler.	Inv. to U.K. 2-10-18. Wounded.
2/Lieut. C.R. Burns.	Inv. to U.K. 4-10-18. Sick.
2/Lieut. F.J. Maybuty.	Died from Wounds. 5-10-18.
2/Lieut. H.R. McCormack.	Inv. to U.K. 2-10-18. Wounded.
2/Lieut. H.G.S. Dannagher.	Inv. to U.K. 2-10-18. Wounded.
Lieut. N.G. Ball.	Reported for Duty. 14-10-18.
2/Lieut. N.P.J. Marsh.	do. do. 13-10-18.
2/Lieut. J. Nichols.	do. do. 13-10-18.
2/Lieut. W.J. Moore.	do. do. 13-10-18.
2/Lieut. W.J. Bunyan.	do. do. 18-10-18.
2/Lieut. N.H. Dunkerton.	do. do. 18-10-18.
2/Lieut. J. Duggan.	do. do. 23-10-18.
2/Lieut. M.J. Gallivan.	do. do. 23-10-18.
2/Lieut. P.J. Murtagh.	do. do. 23-10-18.

STRENGTH.   Officers 40.   Other Ranks. 650.

1st Royal Munster Fusiliers   Page 1.

Army Form C. 2118.

WAR DIARY
or
INTELLIGENCE SUMMARY.
(Erase heading not required.)

HEADQUARTERS
No. ....
2 DEC 1918
1st Battalion
The Royal Munster Fusiliers.

Place	Date	Hour	Summary of Events and Information	Remarks and references to Appendices
TOURBERG de ROUVROY	1918		The Bn. moved from AUSTANG at 0800 hours & arrived at LILLE at 11.40. The Bn. was billeted in a manufactory which had HQ. Quarters, Company, W, X, Y & Z companies	
FIVES			X company was in billets in an adjoining street.	
LILLE	2nd		The morning was spent organizing the Bn. into the new formation of four sections in a platoon. In the afternoon all officers attended a lecture by the Corps Commander.	
"	3rd		Church parade.	
"	4th - 9th		Bn. out doing normal training from 9am to 12 noon. Training consisted of drill, manoeuvre, movements, tactical exercises of companies & platoons.	
"	10th		Church parade.	
"	11th		Bn. out training. Received news of the cessation of hostilities at 11.00 hours this morning.	
"	12th		Bn. full day training following up retiring enemy.	
"	13th		The Divisional Commander inspected the Bn. during the morning.	
"	14th-17th		Bn. carried out the normal training programme.	
"	18th-30th		The Bn. continued training on the same principles. Orders were received for the Bn. to move between ARRAS & proceeds the first week of November.	

M. McKnight Major
1st R. Munster Fusiliers

WAR DIARY or INTELLIGENCE SUMMARY

Army Form C. 2118.

1st Battalion The Royal Munster Fusiliers

Place	Date	Hour	Summary of Events and Information	Remarks and references to Appendices
LILLE	Aug 1918 1/8 2/8		1st Battalion received orders that a Move upto to the 3rd Div was to be made. The day previous was spent in cleaning up Barracks & making preparations for the move.	*
"	3/8		The Battalion paraded at 0800 hours & marched to the Railway Station at MARVIN. There it was entrained at 0930 hours & travelled until 1800 hours for ARRAS.	*
			One march was continued at 1930 hours & the Bn. marched to MAROEUIL & to billets for the night.	
CARVIN	4/8		LENS - VIMY - NEUVILLE - S'VAAST, arriving at 2300 hours. The few days were spent in settling in. The BN. is billeted in two statement camps	*
MAROEUIL	5/8 to 8/8		within the camp & H.Q. & comp. about 1 mile distant. The H. quarters in the village between the two half Bns.	*
	9/8		Bn. training consisted of drill parades, tactical exercise & Exercises on movements connected schemes organised & classes started for men who wished to set up their Trade or profession in civil life.	*
MAROEUIL	15/8 to 17/8 18/8 19/8 20/8		G.O.C. 17th Infantry Bde. inspected the Bn. at 1100 hours Carried out the annual Three mines Division Horse Race, inspection of coat & kits by G.O.C. Division. Training carried out by the Bn. Battalion moved ...	*
	21/8			

WAR DIARY
or
INTELLIGENCE SUMMARY

1st Battalion
The Royal Munster Fusiliers

Place	Date	Hour	Summary of Events and Information	Remarks and references to Appendices
MARŒUIL	24/10		Xmas	
	18/1		Nr Erasmus — Battalion parade 4 [illegible]	
	25		Tactical schemes by Companies. 10 Minenwerfers have [illegible] demolished	
	26		[illegible]	
	27		[illegible] allotted 6 platoon + one to our company every day	
			[illegible] If nothing appears bn reorg. commenced on 30th [illegible]	

E. Monro
LIEUT COL
Commdg. 1st Bn. THE ROYAL MUNSTER FUS

WAR DIARY or INTELLIGENCE SUMMARY

1st R. Munster Fusiliers

Page 1

Place	Date	Hour	Summary of Events and Information	Remarks and references to Appendices
MAROEUIL	1.1.19		57th Divisional Orders re "Demob" & "Work" to be carried out after army reorganisation.	
"	1.19		Kit then 4 returned & for last week on Sat. 29/12.	
"	1.19		The Bn. demands:— 1. To secure their equipment and fulfilment form from transport Reservists:—	
"			1. Rifle — touch up — rub.	
"			2. Full kit & Salvage (area which this forms Salvage works) — once a week.	
"	1.19		3. Battalion roll of transport on R.M.F. Cadre. N.C.O. for Bn Transport — three Sergts in it.	
			Week. Bring Three hours Sergts, Goal machinery, all other 5 hours on the large turn-outs.	
			This after too causes not continuously throughout, in trouble in the situation	
			Who was on duty for the Bn. every three days, the Officer turned on the occasion are as follows:—	
			1. N.C.O. to be working in are D.A.D.S	
			2. A.R.O.A.S then	P.S.O. HARCOURT
			3. N.C.O. & 12 men "	"S" & "Dublin" S.ARTILLERY CORNER
			Owing to work the following details have been employed —	
			N.C.O. & 20 men at LAVEZ N.C.O. & 22 men at Mont S. ELOI	

1ST. BATT. THE ROYAL MUNSTER FUSILIERS.

NUMBERS DEMOBILISED DURING THE MONTH OF JANUARY, 1919.

8. Officers.
166. Other Ranks.

Army Form C. 2118.

1st Bhurlpur Lancers

Page 2

WAR DIARY
or
INTELLIGENCE SUMMARY.
(Erase heading not required.)

Place	Date	Hour	Summary of Events and Information	Remarks and references to Appendices
MARCEUIL	30/9 to 31/9		During the month demobilization has been carried out at an average rate of 45 per week. (For detailed list see Appendix I) Situational state now held throughout the period commencing visit at 70 of the Regiment. This month a decrease to strength 15 at was 13th month. The reduction was due to the demobilization of skilled men of the men composing skilled workman.	

Lt Col H. W. Bhurlpur Major Commdg
1st Bhurlpur Lancers

HEADQUARTERS

No. ....
5ᵗʰ MAR 1919
1st Battalion
The Royal Munster Fusiliers.

WAR DIARY OR INTELLIGENCE SUMMARY.

February 1919 / R. Munster Fus.

Place.	Date.	Hour.	Summary of Events and information.	Remarks references to appendices.
MAROEUIL.	1-3-19		Drill & Training under Company Commanders.	
	2-3-19		Church Parades.	
	3-3-19		Battalion Parade for Training & Musketry.	
	4-3-19		Battalion formed duties, remainder, drill under the R.S.M.	
	5-3-19		Company Training.	
	6-3-19		Battalion Route March.	
	7-3-19		Battalion won Corps Final in the Tug-of-War with both light and heavy teams. Subalterns Officers for training under Captain.P.W.Synott.M.C.	
	8-3-19		Company Training.	
	9-3-19		Church Parades. Battalion found Brigade Duties.	
	10-3-19		Training under Company Commanders.	
	11-3-19		ditto	
	12-3-19		Battalion paraded as strong as possible for Salvage Work.	
	13-3-19		Training under Company Commanders.	
	14-3-19		Battalion Route March.	
	15-3-19		Training under Company Commanders. Battalion found Brigade Duties.	
	16-3-19		Church Parades.	
	17-3-19		Training under Company Commanders.	
	18-3-19		Battalion Drill under the R.S.M.	
	19-3-19		Battalion found the Brigade Duties, remainder training under Company Commanders.	
	20-3-19		Battalion Training for demonstration with Tanks.	
	21-3-19		-ditto-	
	22-3-19		-ditto-	
	23-3-19		Church Parades. Battalion Tug-of-War Teams went to VALENCIENNES to take part in Army Final.	
	24-3-19		Four Officers and 70 Other Ranks proceeded to BRETENCOURT to take part in demonstration with Tanks for Cinema Film. Catchweight Tug-of-War Team beaten in Semi-final for First Army Championship. Heavy Weight Team Won.	
	25-3-19		Heavy Weight Tug of War Team beaten in Final for First Army Championship.	
	26-3-19		—	
	27-3-19		—	
	28-3-19		Battalion won Divisional Platoon Competition and presented with a Silver Bugle and Medals.	

Strength O. Can. 24 Off. 791 other ranks.

57

Army Form C. 2118.

WAR DIARY
or
INTELLIGENCE SUMMARY
(Erase heading not required.)

Army Form 37

1 R. Munster Fus

Place	Date	Hour	Summary of Events and Information	Remarks and references to Appendices
MAROEUIL	1-3-19		Divine Service parades.	
	2.		Working Parties and Training.	
	3.		Company Training.	
	4.		ditto.	
	5.		ditto.	
	6.		Lectures and Company Training.	
	7.		Brigade Working Parties.	
	8.		ditto.	
	9.		C.O's Parade and Company Training	
	10.		ditto.	
	11.		ditto.	
	12.		ditto.	
	13.		Draft proceeded to 7th. Royal Irish Regt.	
	14.		C.O's Parade and Company Training.	
	15.		ditto.	
	16.		ditto. L/Cpl. Warner won heavy weight boxing Competition & Pte. O'Donnell won the Light wt.	
	17.		St. Patrick's Day Mass for the Bn. Sports in the morning and afternoon.	
	18.		Draft left for the 7th. Royal Irish Regt.	
	19.		Company Training.	
	20.		ditto.	
	21.		ditto.	
	22.		ditto.	
	23.		Divine Service Parades.	
	24.		Company Training.	
	25.		Draft proceeded to 7th. Royal Irish Regt.	
	26.		Working Parties.	
	27.		ditto.	
	28.		Companies amalgamate into one Company.	
	29.		Working Parties.	
	30.		Divine Service Parades.	
	31.		Working Parties.	

Holmes Captain.
Commanding 1st. Bn. The Royal Munster Fusiliers.

Army Form C. 2118.

WAR DIARY
or
INTELLIGENCE SUMMARY.

(Erase heading not required.) 1st. Royal Munster Fusiliers

Instructions regarding War Diaries and Intelligence Summaries are contained in F. S. Regs., Part II. and the Staff Manual respectively. Title pages will be prepared in manuscript.

HEADQUARTERS
3 MAY 1919
1st Battalion

Place	Date	Hour	Summary of Events and Information	Remarks and references to Appendices
MAMORUIL.	1-4-1919.		Company Training and Baths.	
	2.		Rifle inspection by the Armr. Sgt. Rifle exercises under Coy. Officers.	
	3.		Company Training.	
	4.		ditto.	
	5.		ditto.	
	6.		Divine Service parades.	
	7.		Fatigue parties for work round the camp.	
	8.		Bn. marched to Baths and then for short route march.	
	9.		Drill under Company Officers.	
	10.		ditto.	
	11.		ditto.	
	12.		All duty men demobilized and remainder are employed men. No men for parades.	
	13.		Divine Service parades.	
	14.		Bn. marched to Baths.	
	15.		------	
	16.		------	
	17.		Bn. Paraded at 10.30 hours for inspection by the Comdg. Officer. Dress- Marching Order	
	18.		------	
	19.		------	
	20.		Divine Service parades.	
	21.		------	
	22.		------	
	23.		------	
	24.		------	
	25.		------	
	26.		------	
	27.		Divine Service Parades.	
	28.		------	
	29.		------	
	30.		------	
			Strength of Battalion 15 Officers. 118 Other Ranks.	

Commanding 1st. Battalion The Royal Munster Fusiliers
Captain.

1st. Bn. The Royal Munster Fusiliers.

WAR DIARY.
or
INTELLIGENCE SUMMARY.

Army Form C.2118.

Place.	Date.	Hour.	Summary of Events and Information.	Remarks references to appendices.
Maroeuil France.	1-5-19 to 31-5-19		Cadre of Battalion waiting to proceed to England. All men employed and no training carried on except by the Regtl. Band who practice daily. Strength of Battalion 13 Officers 89 Other Ranks.	

[signature]
Captain.
Commanding 1st. Bn. The Royal Munster Fusiliers.

HEADQUARTERS
0 MAY 1919
1st Battalion
The Royal Munster Fusiliers.

www.ingramcontent.com/pod-product-compliance
Lightning Source LLC
Chambersburg PA
CBHW081453160426
43193CB00013B/2466